THE QUICK AND EASY
DAILY GRAMMAR WORKBOOK

GRAMMAR ACTIVITIES FOR MIDDLE AND HIGH SCHOOL STUDENTS

by Laura Daly

© Write and Read LLC 2025. All rights reserved.

© Write and Read LLC 2025. All rights reserved. This workbook is for home use or single classroom use, not commercial use or resale. No part of this publication may be reproduced for storage in a retrieval system, or transmitted in any form or by any means—electronic, mechanical, recording, etc.—without the prior written permission of the publisher. Reproduction of these materials for an entire school system is strictly prohibited.

Contact the author:
writeandreadteacher.com
@writeandreadteacher

TABLE OF CONTENTS

Instruction for Use	5
Week 1: Nouns	6-7
Week 2: Commas and Coordinating Conjunctions	8-9
Week 3: Verbs	10-11
Week 4: Capitalization	12-13
Week 5: Pronouns	14-15
Week 6: Subject and Predicate	16-17
Week 7: Independent Clauses	18-19
Week 8: Simple and Compound Sentences	20-21
Week 9: Sentence Fragments and Run-On Sentences	22-23
Week 10: Weeks 1-9 Review	24-25
Week 11: Dependent Clauses	26-27
Week 12: Clauses and Phrases	28-29
Week 13: Complex Sentences	30-31
Week 14: Compound-Complex Sentences	32-33
Week 15: Subject/Verb Agreement	34-35
Week 16: Types of Verbs	36-37
Week 17: Irregular Verbs	38-39
Week 18: Commas 1	40-41
Week 19: Adjectives and Adverbs	42-43
Week 20: Weeks 11-19 Review	44-45
Week 21 41-42: Semicolons	46-47
Week 22: Colons	48-49
Week 23: Quotation Marks	50-51
Week 24: Apostrophes	52-53
Week 25: Commas 2	54-55
Week 26: Parallel Structure	56-57
Week 27: Active vs. Passive Voice	58-59
Week 28: Review Weeks 21-27	60-61
Week 29: Prepositions and Prepositional Phrases	62-63

© Write and Read LLC 2025. All rights reserved.

TABLE OF CONTENTS

Week 30: Modifiers 64-65
Week 31: Prefixes and Suffixes 66-67
Week 32: Homophones 68-69
Week 33: Commonly Misspelled Words 70-71
Week 34: Titles 72-73
Week 35: Weeks 29-34 Review 74-75
Week 36: Whole Year Review 76-77
Answer Keys and Sample Answers 78-93

INSTRUCTIONS FOR USE

This grammar workbook provides 36 weeks of grammar content to review and learn in just a few minutes each day. These quick daily activities are designed to help you build a strong foundation of grammar concepts to become a better reader and writer.

Each week of activities has a different focus topic. You will learn about parts of speech, sentence structures, punctuation, phrases and clauses, and much more. It's important that you cover the topics in order as presented in the book. The content builds on itself, and every nine weeks, there is a review of all the focus topics from the previous eight weeks. The last week of activities is a review of the entire book.

At the back of the book, you will find answer keys and sample answers. If you are a parent working with your child, feel free to tear out the answer keys.

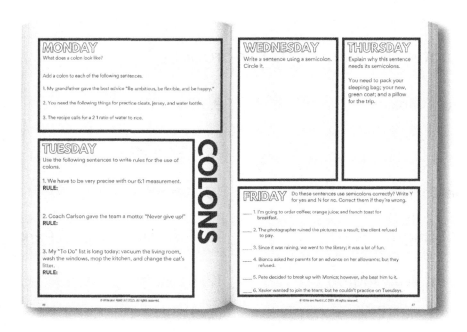

© Write and Read LLC 2025. All rights reserved.

MONDAY

A noun is a word used to identify a person, place, thing, or idea. Circle the nouns from the group of words below.

horse   run   believe   belief   finish   chin   ugly

very   child   bones   I   class   quickly   tried   until

grocery store   weather   hope   silently   textbook

TUESDAY

Common vs. Proper
Common nouns are general things/people/places.
Example: the ocean
Proper nouns refer to specific things/people/places.
Example: the Atlantic Ocean

Label each noun as common (C) or proper (P).

____ 1. Hostess Twinkies

____ 2. book

____ 3. chameleon

____ 4. Lake Michigan

____ 5. President Washington

____ 6. teacher

____ 7. Chicago

____ 8. city

____ 9. Mr. Baker

____ 10. hotel

____ 11. Yosemite National Park

____ 12. trails

____ 13. doctor

____ 14. Canada

NOUNS

WEDNESDAY

Concrete nouns refer to actual things/people/places. Example: house
Abstract nouns refer to ideas. Example: love

Label each noun as concrete (C) or abstract (A).

____ 1. honesty   ____ 7. hope

____ 2. desk   ____ 8. plate

____ 3. river   ____ 9. mother

____ 4. sadness   ____ 10. school

____ 5. iPad   ____ 11. liberty

____ 6. hand   ____ 12. faith

THURSDAY

Write 1-2 sentences using each type of noun. Label each noun.

_____
_____
_____
_____
_____
_____
_____
_____
_____
_____

FRIDAY

Identify each noun in the sentences below.

Callie walked down to the beach, shuffling through the sand. She carried her towel and bag in her left hand. Squinting against the sun, she looked for a shady spot to sit down. Finding one, she dropped her stuff and ran to the lake.

COMMAS and COORDINATING CONJUNCTIONS

MONDAY

A coordinating conjunction is a word that connects words, phrases, or clauses. There are seven coordinating conjunctions. The ones most commonly used are *and*, *but*, and *or*. Add a coordinating conjunction that makes sense in the sentence below.

1. The students got everything done in class, _____ they didn't have any homework.

2. Molly fell down the stairs, _____ she broke her leg.

3. I wanted to buy chocolate ice cream, _____ the store was out.

TUESDAY

Coordinating conjunctions can be used with a comma to connect independent clauses. The comma goes at the end of the first independent clause and before the coordinating conjunction.

Ex. My mother loves to garden, for she finds it peaceful.

Directions: Add commas where needed in the following sentences. Not all sentences need a comma.

1. You can go swimming or to the movies.

2. The zoo was packed so we went to the aquarium instead.

3. Frank wants Red Hot Cheetos but Gabby ate all of them.

4. Chris has a cat and two dogs.

5. She waited for the bus yet it was late again.

6. Harper arrived first and she helped me finish decorating.

© Write and Read LLC 2025. All rights reserved.

WEDNESDAY

Write your own sentence using a comma and coordinating conjunction correctly. Circle your comma and coordinating conjunction.

_____
_____
_____
_____
_____
_____
_____
_____
_____

THURSDAY

List the 7 coordinating conjunctions:

F

A

N

B

O

Y

S

FRIDAY

Label each sentence as correct (C) or incorrect (I). If it's incorrect, fix it.

____ 1. Derrick tossed the football and Carson caught it.

____ 2. It was the first day of school, so the school was full of lost students

____ 3. Hide and Seek is Cece's favorite game but, she's not very good at it.

____ 4. The cat jumped off the couch and ran away.

____ 5. Tony wandered the halls, for he didn't want to go to class.

____ 6. Andrea walked home but Steven rode his bike.

MONDAY

A verb is a word that is used to describe an action or state of being. Circle the verbs from the group of words below.

hear   vein   return   exit   school   accepted   might

verse   remains   in   quieted   windy   credit   stride

build   the   honor   songs   people   wash   trains

TUESDAY

Circle each verb in the sentences below.

The wind howled, and rain pelted her, making her shiver.

She dashed up the stairs and banged on the door. "I

hope someone answers," she thought. As she shivered

on the porch, she made a promise to herself. "I will find

my mother someday."

© Write and Read LLC 2025. All rights reserved.

WEDNESDAY

Some words can be nouns or verbs depending on the context. Determine whether each bolded word is being used as a verb (V) or a noun (N).

____ 1. The dogs **watch** the children with malice.

____ 2. Susie took her time with her **climb** up the mountain.

____ 3. I need that **plant** for the party tomorrow.

____ 4. They will **remain** at home until tomorrow.

____ 5. The students **graduated** at the end of the year.

____ 6. The **stay** at the hotel was wonderful.

THURSDAY

Write 1-2 sentences using verbs in at least two different tenses. Identify each verb and label the tense you used.

FRIDAY

Verbs have three tenses: past, present, and future. Complete the chart by writing the proper tense for each verb.

Past	Present	Future
	learn	
pushed		
		will start
	cook	

MONDAY

Correct the capitalization error(s) in each sentence. Use the correct editing marks. (Place three lines underneath a letter to capitalize it or a slash through the letter to make it lowercase.)

1. our trip to chicago was postponed after our flight from france was canceled.

2. Whenever Jaime called, officer Charles picked right up.

3. My english class was watching a movie that my Mother didn't approve of.

TUESDAY

Make a list of four capitalization rules with an example for each.

1.

2.

3.

4.

CAPITALIZATION

WEDNESDAY

When writing titles, you capitalize the first, last, and all important words. Rewrite each title and capitalize the titles correctly.

1. the wind in the willows

2. the perks of being a wallflower

3. the catcher in the rye

THURSDAY

Write 1-2 sentences using at least 3 different capitalization rules.

FRIDAY

For each number, choose which sentence is capitalized correctly by placing an X on the line provided.

1. _____ Where is the President?

   _____ Where is the president?

2. _____ We'll go visit Lake Michigan this summer.

   _____ We'll go visit lake Michigan this summer.

3. _____ Maddie's taking english and french this year.

   _____ Maddie's taking English and French this year.

© Write and Read LLC 2025. All rights reserved.

MONDAY

Pronouns replace nouns. Choose the correct pronoun to complete each sentence. Circle your answers.

1. The computer lost (his / its) charge.

2. Ian mowed (his / him) neighbor's lawn.

3. My friend and (I / me) marched in the parade.

4. (We / Us) like to go out to eat for special occasions.

5. The dogs need (their / them) water dish refilled.

TUESDAY

The antecedent of the pronoun is the noun the pronoun replaces.

Example: Amy ate her apple. (Her replaces Amy, so Amy is the antecedent.)

Underline the antecedent in each of the following sentences.

1. My mother and I took our pets to the vet.

2. Nathan invited his friend over after school.

3. The team won their first game.

4. Arnold, you need to get to work.

5. The members of Congress spoke to their constituents.

6. Andre lost his new sweatshirt at school.

7. After leaving, Mia and Emma walked to their grandma's house.

PRONOUNS

© Write and Read LLC 2025. All rights reserved.

WEDNESDAY

Subject pronouns complete an action. Object pronouns receive action.

Example: I hugged him. (I is a subject pronoun completing an action. Him is the object pronoun receiving the action.)

Make a list of all of the pronouns you can think of below and label them as Subject or Object.

Subject	Object

THURSDAY

Write a sentence that uses at least one pronoun. Label the pronoun and the antecedent.

FRIDAY

The pronoun and antecedent below don't match. Change each pronoun to correct the sentences.

1. The **dogs** chewed <u>its</u> bone. _____

2. **Holly** ran to <u>his</u> home. _____

3. The **desk** was wobbly after <u>our</u> leg broke. _____

4. **I** asked <u>us</u> principal for help. _____

5. The **firefighters** wanted to update <u>my</u> firetruck. _____

6. **Mr. Miller** asked for <u>its</u> rake back. _____

MONDAY

The subject of a sentence is the noun/pronoun completing an action. Circle the subject in each sentence.

1. The big black dog chased after the ball.

2. Sam watches the baseball game on TV.

3. Jadan, my best friend, wants to go to the movies.

TUESDAY

The predicate of a sentence is the action and any description of the action.
Ex. **My mother** wanted to know where I was going.
"My mother" is the subject, and "wanted to know where I was going" is the predicate. "Wanted" is the main verb, and the rest enhances the verb. Underline the predicate in the following sentences.

1. The novel ended with a twist.

2. Polly the parakeet flew through the enclosure, looking for a place to land.

3. Eventually, our class will finish the final project.

4. The earthquake rattled the windows.

SUBJECT and PREDICATE

WEDNESDAY

Write your own sentence. Circle the subject and underline the predicate.

THURSDAY

In your own words, state what the subject and predicate of a sentence are.

FRIDAY

Add a subject or predicate to the following sentences.

1. _____ bought apples and milk at the store.

2. _____ will call once the surgery is over.

3. Bobby's big sister _____.

4. The prickly cactus _____.

MONDAY

Independent clause: The cars raced around the track.

NOT an independent clause: Raced around the track.
Since the cars raced around the track.

Write your own definition of an independent clause below. (What does it have? What does it do?)

TUESDAY

Label each group of words as an independent clause (I) or not an independent clause (N).

___ 1. Written by Harper Lee.

___ 2. I enjoyed that book.

___ 3. Many movers and shakers like this place.

___ 4. Because we left early.

___ 5. The janitors cleaned up quickly.

___ 6. Before the show had ended.

___ 7. Practice starts in an hour.

___ 8. I always carry a water bottle.

___ 9. Since she left the party.

___ 10. The children played tag.

INDEPENDENT CLAUSES

WEDNESDAY

Explain why the following is or isn't an independent clause.

If I had a million dollars.

THURSDAY

Write your own independent clause.

FRIDAY

Turn the following groups of words into independent clauses.

1. The great debate.
   _____

2. After her tantrum.
   _____

3. Breaking down the boxes.
   _____

4. Since she read the book.
   _____

MONDAY

Simple Sentence: The dog chased the cat.

Compound Sentence: The train was long, yet we weren't late because of it.

What makes a simple sentence?

What makes a compound sentence?

TUESDAY

Label each sentence as simple (**S**) or compound (**C**).

____ 1. Annie got into her first choice college, and she got a full ride scholarship.

____ 2. Jocelyn's graduation party was rainy and cold.

____ 3. Trent plays on the basketball team but hates it.

____ 4. Beatrice wanted to go swimming; Hank wanted to go biking.

____ 5. The weather was terrible, so our flight was delayed.

____ 6. I let the dogs out last night.

____ 7. Portia got the lead role, and everyone was jealous.

____ 8. Many of the students were late to school.

____ 9. She bought apples and oranges at the store.

SIMPLE and COMPOUND SENTENCES

WEDNESDAY

Write your own simple and compound sentences.

SIMPLE:

COMPOUND:

THURSDAY

What punctuation can be used to combine two independent clauses into a compound sentence?

FRIDAY

Are these compound sentences punctuated correctly? Answer Y for yes or N for no. Fix the incorrect sentences.

____ 1. Cal asked Patrice out but she said no.

____ 2. Vinnie lost his keys at the library; thankfully, a good samaritan turned them in.

____ 3. The restaurant was closed, we went somewhere else.

____ 4. Jesus made the baseball team his freshman year his family was very proud.

____ 5. You can go first, and then I'll take a turn.

MONDAY

Sentence Fragment: Walked up the stairs.

Run-on Sentence: Brenda wrecked her car she had to take the bus.

What is a sentence fragment?

What is a run-on sentence?

TUESDAY

Identify each of the following as a sentence fragment (SF) or a run-on (RO).

____ 1. Planted the flowers.

____ 2. Before running our errands.

____ 3. Lauren graduated college now she's looking for a full time job.

____ 4. Grant couldn't find the bus stop, he called an Uber instead.

____ 5. Lena finally.

____ 6. The fire alarm went off so the class filed outside quickly and quietly.

____ 7. He wanted to win the race he knew it would be difficult.

____ 8. After leaving the art show on Saturday.

SENTENCE FRAGMENTS and RUN-ON SENTENCES

WEDNESDAY

Fix the following run-on sentence. Explain why it needed to be fixed.

Zane slid to home plate the catcher got him out.

THURSDAY

Fix the following sentence fragment. Explain how you fixed it.

Through the neighborhood.

FRIDAY

Identify each of the following as a sentence fragment (SF), a run-on (RO), or correct (C).

____ 1. Ari loves to go to the library; she loves to play, color, and check out books.

____ 2. Tonya texted me back but I ignored her.

____ 3. Partied all night.

____ 4. The house down the street.

____ 5. Judy asked for help and received it.

____ 6. Walter missed the delivery, he had to go to the post office to get it.

MONDAY

Add a subject to the following sentences.

1. _____ produced a lot of noise.

2. _____ counted too fast.

Add a predicate to the following sentences.

3. The cat on the mat _____.

4. Our first plan _____.

TUESDAY

Match each grammar concept to its best description.

a. noun   d. independent clause
b. subject   e. simple sentence
c. predicate   f. compound sentence

____ 1. has a subject and predicate

____ 2. sentence with two independent clauses

____ 3. person, place, thing, or idea

____ 4. the noun/pronoun completing the action in a sentence

____ 5. the action and description of action in a sentence

____ 6. sentence with one independent clause

WEEKS 1-9 REVIEW

WEDNESDAY

Write a compound sentence using a comma and coordinating conjunction.

THURSDAY

Circle the nouns and underline the verbs in the following sentences.

Gary handed Susan the umbrella when it started to rain. Susan smiled and thanked him. Gary smiled back.

FRIDAY

Label each group of words as a simple sentence (**S**), compound sentence (**C**), or sentence fragment (**F**).

____ 1. I made a grocery list; then my husband did the shopping.

____ 2. A plan.

____ 3. You tried.

____ 4. The trip was long and complicated, but they finally made it.

____ 5. The pool needed to be filled and cleaned.

____ 6. The scared cat hid from the children.

MONDAY

What's an independent clause?

Based on that, what do you think a **dependent** clause is?

Label whether each group of words is dependent or not. (Y or N)

____ 1. Since we left

____ 2. However, I wanted to go

____ 3. Before the game ends

TUESDAY

Subordinating conjunctions keep independent clauses from being independent (making them dependent). There are too many to memorize, but they leave you with a question.

Ex. **If** I had a million dollars (**If** is the subordinating conjunction.)

Underline the subordinating conjunction in each sentence.

1. After Carla failed her test, she asked if she could retake it.

2. The football game was canceled since a thunderstorm rolled in.

3. The students voted to read outside because the weather was finally nice.

4. Even though the team lost, everyone was proud of the players' progress.

5. The receptionist will keep your ID until you return.

DEPENDENT CLAUSES

WEDNESDAY

Write your own dependent clause. Circle the subordinating conjunction.

THURSDAY

Explain why this is a dependent clause.

Whenever she calls.

FRIDAY

Identify whether each group of words is an independent (I) or dependent (D) clause.

____ 1. Since you've been gone

____ 2. The cat ran away

____ 3. Sam and Stacy took your things to the office

____ 4. Unless she tells the truth

____ 5. If you get here before 10 a.m.

____ 6. After he gets home

MONDAY

What do independent and dependent clauses have in common?

Phrases don't have both of these; sometimes they have neither.

Do you think the following groups of words are a phrase, yes or no?

____1. Hounded by paparazzi.

____2. I called yesterday.

TUESDAY

Identify each group of words as a clause (**C**) or a phrase (**P**).

____ 1. Before long.

____ 2. Because I said so.

____ 3. He pretended not to hear her.

____ 4. Neither one of us.

____ 5. Baked into the crust.

____ 6. After an hour.

____ 7. She watched him silently.

____ 8. While Norah napped.

____ 9. It was her only purse.

CLAUSES and PHRASES

WEDNESDAY

Write your own phrase and explain what keeps it from being a clause.

THURSDAY

Circle the phrase and underline the clause in this sentence.

In the beginning, Carla didn't need help.

FRIDAY

Identify each group of words as an independent clause (I), dependent clause (D), or phrase (P).

____ 1. The broken computer.

____ 2. Although I don't know.

____ 3. Since it's the end.

____ 4. We left after school yesterday.

____ 5. In the morning.

____ 6. Julio called out to her.

MONDAY

What makes a simple sentence?

What makes a compound sentence?

Complex Sentence: Whenever he calls, she lets it go to voicemail.
What makes a complex sentence?

TUESDAY

Label whether each of the following is complex or not. Write Y for yes and N for no.

____ 1. Nikki needed new clothes since she switched jobs.

____ 2. After Pete couldn't find it, his mother found it in two minutes.

____ 3. The student plagiarized his paper.

____ 4. Alex left before the party was over.

____ 5. Wendy and Violet tried out for the cheerleading team after school.

____ 6. After the game, everyone went out for pizza.

____ 7. During the intermission, Jay bought some candy.

COMPLEX SENTENCES

WEDNESDAY

Write your own complex sentence. Circle your dependent clause, and underline your independent clause.

THURSDAY

Circle the dependent clause, and underline the independent clause.

Betty's mother forced her to go though she didn't want to.

FRIDAY

If the dependent clause comes BEFORE the independent clause, set it off with a comma. If the dependent clause comes AFTER the independent clause, no comma is needed.

Determine whether the sentences below are punctuated correctly. (Y or N)

____ 1. Because Adam failed, he had to retake the class.

____ 2. Cammie wanted to swim, hike, and bike when her family vacationed on the lake.

____ 3. As much as Romeo loves racing he's not very good at it.

____ 4. You'll be late if you miss the bus.

____ 5. He never picked up the groceries, since his car broke down.

MONDAY

Based on what you know about other types of sentences? What do you think makes a compound-complex sentence?

Sample compound-complex sentence: When Gnomeo and Juliet met, they fell in love; then they realized they came from opposite families.

TUESDAY

Label whether each of the following is compound-complex or not. Write Y for yes and N for no.

____ 1. Harvey asked Sabrina out for coffee, but she said no.

____ 2. Sebastian tried to convince Ariel since he was afraid of the king; he failed.

____ 3. After winter arrived early, people worried magic was involved.

____ 4. Although Polly was favored to win, Nick took home the trophy, so there were a lot of tears.

____ 5. The zoo was closed, but we still wanted to do something fun since it was the weekend.

____ 6. Since the argument, Joy has been avoiding me.

COMPOUND-COMPLEX SENTENCES

WEDNESDAY

Write your own compound-complex sentence. Circle your dependent clause(s), and underline your independent clauses.

THURSDAY

Is the following sentence punctuated correctly? Explain.

I wanted to go to the lake even though it was cold but no one would go with me.

FRIDAY

Label each sentence as simple (**S**), compound (**C**), complex (**CX**), or compound-complex (**CC**).

____ 1. Unless Patrick arrives soon, we'll have to leave without him; I'm sorry.

____ 2. The carpet was still wet from being steamed.

____ 3. Her frog friend helped her find a costume, but it wasn't enough to truly disguise her.

____ 4. Since it finally stopped raining, Kevin's going to mow the grass.

____ 5. Trevor wandered the halls until the bell rang.

____ 6. Tiffany stuffed envelopes while Greg stamped them, but they're still behind schedule.

MONDAY

Circle the correct version of the verb to complete the sentence.

1. The statue (speaks/speak) to the gnome.

2. They (thinks/think) that the end of the movie was bad.

3. I (believes/believe) chocolate is better than vanilla.

4. The class (prefers/prefer) last quarter's book over this one.

5. Your purple socks (smells/smell) after gym class.

TUESDAY

Subject/verb agreement means that you're using the correct version of the verb for your noun/pronoun. For instance, singular nouns need the singular version of the verb, and plural nouns needs plural versions.

Do the following sentences have correct subject/verb agreement? Write Y for yes and N for no.

____ 1. Writers enjoy when their books are published.

____ 2. Pounds of butter melts in the sun.

____ 3. Many of the others want the class to be over.

____ 4. The duck and the goose swims in the lake.

____ 5. My mother or my brother pick me up after school.

____ 6. My dad makes the best chicken noodle soup.

SUBJECT/VERB AGREEMENT

WEDNESDAY

Write your own sentence in present tense. Explain why you need to use that version of the verb.

THURSDAY

Does the following sentence have correct subject/verb agreement? Explain.

Sarah want her husband back.

FRIDAY

The following sentences have issues with subject/verb agreement. Fix them, keeping the verbs in PRESENT tense. Write the verb correctly on the line.

1. Greece look beautiful this time of year. _____

2. You needs to complete your assignment. _____

3. Taylor or Violet exit the auditorium first. _____

4. Crafting the perfect response require diligence and patience. _____

5. The charger always die after I use it. _____

6. They wants a new laptop computer. _____

TYPES OF VERBS

MONDAY

Linking Verbs connect the subject to a noun or adjective that renames/describes the subject.

Ex. Antonio **became** a star football player.

Circle the linking verb in each sentence.

1. The game appeared over.

2. Grandma's cooking smells delicious.

3. The dog is in trouble.

TUESDAY

Action verbs express action or possession.
Example: Wanda **chases** the cat.

Circle the action verb in each sentence.

1. The track team ran at practice.

2. The postman delivered the mail.

Helping verbs are used with other verbs to show extra information (possibility or time). The helping verb and action/linking verb together are known as a **verb phrase**.
Example: His friends (are) **planning** a surprise party.

Underline the verb phrase and circle the helping verb.

3. The birds might build a nest here again.

4. Olive is obsessed with her stuffed dog.

WEDNESDAY

Write your own sentence using a helping verb, and circle the verb phrase.

THURSDAY

Identify the verb type and explain your answer.

Bobby is a fan of the NFL.

FRIDAY

Identify each bolded verb/verb phrase as linking (**L**), action (**A**), or helping (**H**).

____ 1. We **ought to return** the library books today.

____ 2. The clown **looked** like a fool.

____ 3. The email **stated** the manager's expectations.

____ 4. Elsa **felt** relief once the truth was uncovered.

____ 5. They **were gardening** before you arrived.

____ 6. Jason **threw** the football to the receiver.

MONDAY

Irregular verbs are verbs that don't follow the normal pattern of adding "ed" to the end of the verb to make it past tense.

Circle the irregular verbs. (They're in present tense, so think about what the word would look like in past tense.)

start   begin   yell   is   live   bounce   call

know   birth   love   pour   run   steal   swim

TUESDAY

Circle the irregular verb(s) in each sentence.

1. The television broke after the storm.

2. The students read silently yesterday.

3. The neighborhood woke up because of the fireworks.

4. The park ranger led the way down the path.

5. Heidi blew out the candles before she left.

6. Connie felt bad for the rude comments she made.

7. I see the baby has fallen asleep.

8. Claire was the first to sing in the talent show.

IRREGULAR VERBS

WEDNESDAY

Write a sentence using an irregular verb in present tense. Circle it.

Now, write the same sentence in past tense.

THURSDAY

Complete each sentence with an irregular verb.

1. The birds _____

a nest against the house.

2. The baby _____

near her mom.

FRIDAY

Put each of the following irregular verbs into past tense.

1. are _____

2. cut _____

3. sell _____

4. sleep _____

5. take _____

6. win _____

7. buy _____

8. catch _____

9. drink _____

10. find _____

11. pay _____

12. steal _____

MONDAY

Write three basic comma rules and give an example of each.

1.

2.

3.

TUESDAY

Add or delete one comma in each of the following sentences.

1. The Declaration of Independence was adopted on July 4, 1776 which makes it an important day in US history.

2. I want to go to Los Angeles California one day.

3. The black fluffy dog was very friendly.

4. As I read the sign, I realized we need to stop for gas, before we cross the long bridge.

5. Natalie was really excited about the party so she invited extra people.

6. Although I understood the directions I did not follow them.

COMMAS 1

WEDNESDAY

Write a sentence that uses at least two commas correctly.

THURSDAY

What comma rule is used in this sentence?

Portia needed a teal, sparkly dress for the event.

FRIDAY

Choose the sentence punctuated correctly by placing an X on the line.

1. _____ Bobby's license says his birthdate is September 15, 2002 but he's always told me his birthday is the 16th.
   _____ Bobby's license says his birthdate is September 15, 2002, but he's always told me his birthday is the 16th.

2. _____ Though Charlotte is from Baton Rouge, Louisiana, you'd never know it from the way she talks.
   _____ Though Charlotte is from Baton Rouge, Louisiana you'd never know it from the way she talks.

3. _____ Violet wants an updated cell phone.
   _____ Violet wants an updated, cell phone.

MONDAY

An **adjective** modifies/describes nouns. An **adverb** modifies/describes adjectives, verbs, and adverbs.

Circle any adjectives and adverbs in each sentence.

1. The old man walked tiredly down the stairs.

2. Tomorrow, Ronnie will pick up the puppy.

3. Alejandro ran quickly around the track.

4. The blue sky was clear.

5. Wren sang beautifully.

TUESDAY

Identify whether each bolded word is an adjective (adj) or adverb (adv).

_____ 1. The **brick** house crumbled around us.

_____ 2. The brown pony walked **briskly** through the pen.

_____ 3. It was **very** cold last night.

_____ 4. Bonnie's **blue** eyes were clear and bright.

_____ 5. Connie is so **tall** she had to duck on the playground.

_____ 6. They left **quietly** after the argument.

_____ 7. The little boy cried **softly** into his pillow.

_____ 8. The **pale** boy said he wasn't feeling well.

ADJECTIVES and ADVERBS

WEDNESDAY

Write your own sentence using an adjective and adverb. Circle the adjective and underline the adverb.

THURSDAY

Is the bolded word an adjective or adverb, and what is it modifying in the sentence?

The sun was **really** bright today.

FRIDAY

Circle the correct word to complete the sentence.

1. He spoke (good/well) during his speech.

2. Tommy was really (bad/badly) at tennis.

3. Valerie acted (real/really) well.

4. The food tasted (good/well).

5. The cords were fraying (bad/badly).

What do you notice about when to use good vs. well and bad vs. badly?

MONDAY

Label each bolded verb as action (**A**), linking (**L**), or helping (**H**).

____ 1. The library books **were due** yesterday.

____ 2. The bus **stopped** quickly.

____ 3. Robin **appeared** sad.

____ 4. The magician **pulls** a rabbit from his hat.

____ 5. The restaurant **has added** several tables due to its popularity.

____ 6. Lauren **is** my best friend.

TUESDAY

Match each grammar concept to its best description.

a. adjective
b. adverb
c. compound-complex sentence
d. complex sentence
e. dependent clause
f. phrase

____ 1. has a subject and predicate but can't stand alone as a sentence

____ 2. a sentence with one independent clause and at least one dependent clause

____ 3. doesn't have a subject and predicate

____ 4. describes/modifies verbs, adjectives, adverbs

____ 5. a sentence with at least two independent clauses and one dependent clause

____ 6. describes/modifies nouns and pronouns

WEEKS 11-19 REVIEW

WEDNESDAY

Write your own complex or compound-complex sentence. Label it.

THURSDAY

Correct each sentence.

1. The dog or the cat need to ride in the backseat.

2. The dogs barks loudly.

3. The cat cry when it is cold.

FRIDAY

Choose the correct sentence by placing an X on the line.

1. _____ The table breaked after the heavy wooden fan fell on it.
   _____ The table broke after the heavy, wooden fan fell on it.

2. _____ April 15, is Tax Day in the US, but my mother and father forgets every year.
   _____ April 15 is Tax Day in the US, but my mother and father forget every year.

3. _____ His uncle asked for his help after school, though he had other plans, he said okay.
   _____ His uncle asked for his help after school; though he had other plans, he said okay.

MONDAY

1. What does a semicolon look like?

2. What is the semicolon doing in this sentence?
The dance is this weekend; however, she's grounded.

TUESDAY

Semicolons can be used to combine independent clauses (with or without a conjunctive adverb like "however") and in lists where the items contain commas. Add at least one semicolon to each of the following sentences.

1. I'd like to visit Los Angeles, California Seattle, Washington and Phoenix, Arizona next summer.

2. When we finally leave, please call your uncle he's going to be worried.

3. Josh is getting his first dog therefore, he needs a lot of new supplies.

4. Chris came home early his car got a flat tire.

5. I need eggs, for your breakfast tomorrow fish; and butter, in case ours is melted.

SEMICOLONS

WEDNESDAY

Write a sentence using a semicolon. Circle it.

THURSDAY

Explain why this sentence needs its semicolons.

You need to pack your sleeping bag; your new, green coat; and a pillow for the trip.

FRIDAY

Do these sentences use semicolons correctly? Write Y for yes and N for no. Correct them if they're wrong.

___ 1. I'm going to order coffee; orange juice; and french toast for breakfast.

___ 2. The photographer ruined the pictures as a result; the client refused to pay.

___ 3. Since it was raining, we went to the library; it was a lot of fun.

___ 4. Bianca asked her parents for an advance on her allowance; but they refused.

___ 5. Pete decided to break up with Monica; however, she beat him to it.

___ 6. Xavier wanted to join the team; but he couldn't practice on Tuesdays.

MONDAY

What does a colon look like?

Add a colon to each of the following sentences.

1. My grandfather gave the best advice "Be ambitious, be flexible, and be happy."

2. You need the following things for practice cleats, jersey, and water bottle.

3. The recipe calls for a 2 1 ratio of water to rice.

TUESDAY

Use the following sentences to write rules for the use of colons.

1. We have to be very precise with our 6:1 measurement.
RULE:

2. Coach Carlson gave the team a motto: "Never give up!"
RULE:

3. My "To Do" list is long today: vacuum the living room, wash the windows, mop the kitchen, and change the cat's litter.
RULE:

COLONS

WEDNESDAY

Write your own sentence using a colon. Circle it.

THURSDAY

What colon rule is used here?

It's important to remember everything: your passport, money, and itinerary.

FRIDAY

Which sentence is written correctly? Place an X on the line to mark the sentence that is correct.

1. _____ You need: notebooks, pencils, and folders.
   _____ You need to take the following things: notebooks, pencils, and folders.

2. _____ He yelled, "I love you!"
   _____ He yelled; "I love you!"

3. _____ I tell my students this all the time; "Following directions is a life skill."
   _____ I tell my students this all the time: "Following directions is a life skill."

MONDAY

When do you use quotation marks?

Add quotation marks to the following sentences.

1. Mr. Barkley yelled, Get out of my garden!

2. I'm afraid the kitchen is closed, the waiter told us.

3. Destiny explained, A mouse chewed through the wires.

TUESDAY

Dialogue tags are used to tell the reader who's speaking and how it's being said. These should be set off with a comma. Add a comma where needed in the following sentences.

1. The director barked "Get out here this instant!"

2. "The show must go on" he declared.

The start of dialogue should always be capitalized; it's like the beginning of a sentence. Capitalize what's needed in the following sentences.

3. "please," wanda pleaded, "don't leave me here."

4. Chester called, "come here, kitty."

QUOTATION MARKS

WEDNESDAY

Write your own line of dialogue using correct punctuation.

THURSDAY

Should other punctuation marks at the end of quotation marks go inside or outside the marks? Why?

FRIDAY

If you're using just a small piece of a quote (a few words), you don't have to capitalize the first word of the quote. Determine whether each sentence below is written correctly. Write Y for yes and N for no.

____ 1. Katrina's "Too little, too late" attitude was annoying after Joyce worked so hard.

____ 2. The cashier asked, "Do you have a coupon for that?"

____ 3. The teacher called "Mason" from the back of the room.

____ 4. "Whatever you want," Oscar cried," Just don't take my bird!"

____ 5. Mario's use of air quotes for "fire hazard" showed us he didn't take it seriously.

MONDAY

Apostrophes are used to show possession. Most of the time, you should use **'s** to show possession. If a proper noun ends in **s** and has two or more syllables, just add an apostrophe to the end of the word. A one syllable proper noun that ends in **s** can still use **'s** at the end. For a singular common noun ending in **s**, use **'s**. A plural common noun ending in **s** would just use an apostrophe at the end.

Add an apostrophe in the correct spot to the following words to show possession.

1. the choir
2. princess
3. classes
4. Anna
5. parents
6. horse
7. team
8. boss
9. Mr. Wells
10. men
11. princesses
12. Mrs. Reynolds

TUESDAY

Contractions combine two words into one using an apostrophe. What two words form the following contractions?

1. It's _____ + _____
2. Couldn't _____ + _____
3. Won't _____ + _____
4. I'm _____ + _____
5. They've _____ + _____
6. Y'all _____ + _____
7. She'd _____ + _____
8. You've _____ + _____
9. We'd _____ + _____
10. Haven't _____ + _____

APOSTROPHES

WEDNESDAY

Write two of your own sentences using apostrophes to show possession.

THURSDAY

Write the contraction for each set of words.

1. are + not

2. he + is

3. will + not

4. I + will

5. would + not

6. we + will

FRIDAY

Do the following sentences use apostrophes correctly? Write Y for yes and N for no.

____ 1. Heathers' mom said she can't go.

____ 2. I cann't wait for the weekend!

____ 3. You'll have to log in again.

____ 4. Don't worry about it.

____ 5. Brutus' betrayal of Caesar probably hurt the most.

____ 6. Lets' go out for dinner tonight.

MONDAY

Write a comma rule for each sentence below.

1. My teacher, the one with the hamster, is my favorite.
RULE:

2. First, turn in your assignment.
RULE:

3. You know, however, that she disagrees.
RULE:

TUESDAY

Are the following sentences punctuated correctly? Write Y for yes and N for no. Fix any incorrect sentences.

____ 1. Consequently you didn't get the job.

____ 2. Little Women, my favorite book, is by Louisa May Alcott.

____ 3. One at a time, the students lined up for lunch.

____ 4. She wondered however, if anyone else knew.

____ 5. Patty, the one with the new car wants to hire a new maid.

____ 6. Like I said no you didn't get the job.

____ 7. Leah, the girl with the ponytail is a great diver.

COMMAS 2

WEDNESDAY

Write your own sentence using one of the comma rules from this week.

THURSDAY

What comma rule from this week is used here?

The new student, Taylor, needs somewhere to sit.

FRIDAY

Add any missing commas in the following sentences.

1. In addition make sure you correct the following issues.

2. Our waiter the one with the long hair is over by the kitchen.

3. Plenty of people in fact don't believe it.

4. You and I therefore are no longer friends.

5. Yesterday the cat ran away.

6. Chris Evans who played Captain America in the Marvel movies is his favorite actor.

MONDAY

Parallel structure, or parallelism, is using the same grammatical structure in similar clauses and phrases. This creates balance in the sentence and makes it easier to read and understand. Choose the sentence that uses correct parallel structure. Place an X on the line.

1. _____ I need to buy groceries, stopping by the post office, and returned library books.

   _____ I need to buy groceries, stop by the post office, and return library books.

2. _____ The girl sang beautifully and clearly.

   _____ The girl sang beautifully and also clearly.

3. _____ When she called, he will let me know.

   _____ When she called, he let me know.

TUESDAY

Rewrite each sentence to correct the issue with parallel structure.

1. Carlos would like a new phone and to buy a new tablet.

2. Vanessa hates to run and swimming.

3. Carrot is an older cat and also orange.

4. Abby likes reading books, to build with blocks, and singing the ABC's.

PARALLEL STURCTURE

WEDNESDAY

Write your own sentence that uses correct parallel structure.

THURSDAY

Explain what parallel structure is in your own words.

FRIDAY

Determine whether the sentence is written correctly. Write Y for yes and N for no. Correct any errors in the sentences.

____ 1. Her cousin enjoys hiking at the Dunes and to swim in Lake Michigan.

____ 2. Violet is a skilled painter and is an avid reader.

____ 3. Clifford ran quickly and quietly down the hall.

____ 4. Bob practices on Tuesdays, Thursdays, and on a Saturday.

____ 5. Either go to the dance or the party.

____ 6. Ollie loves cupcakes, cookies, and he loves pies.

MONDAY

Active voice is when the subject is doing the action. Passive voice is when the subject receives the action. Label each as active (**A**) or passive (**P**).

___ 1. The computer updates automatically.

___ 2. The play will be reviewed by the critics.

___ 3. The crackers were crushed.

___ 4. The pilot announced our arrival.

___ 5. The officer directed traffic after the concert.

TUESDAY

Passive voice is a verb phrase that contains a "be" verb and a past participle verb (usually ending in -ed or -en). Rewrite the sentence to change the passive verbs to active.

1. The house **was cleaned** before being sold.

2. The puzzle pieces **were lost** when putting it away.

Rewrite the sentence to change the active verbs to passive.

3. UberEats **delivered** our dinner.

4. The plane **took off** almost an hour late.

ACTIVE & PASSIVE VOICE

WEDNESDAY

Write your own sentence and identify whether you're using active or passive voice.

THURSDAY

Is the following sentence active or passive? Explain how you know.

Barbara felt tired after the game.

FRIDAY

Active sentences are more direct and often less confusing. Passive sentences are better when the subject is unknown or unimportant.

Which version of the sentence is better for the situation?

1. _____ My brother invited me to his wedding.
   _____ I was invited by my brother to his wedding.

2. _____ Someone robbed our house last night.
   _____ Our house was robbed last night.

3. _____ Walter needs to buy new school supplies.
   _____ New school supplies are needed by Walter.

MONDAY

Match each sentence with its comma rule.
a. appositive phrase   b. introductory words/phrases
c. interrupting word

____ 1. I don't believe, however, that you're correct.

____ 2. First, we need to decide who's driving with who.

____ 3. Without her, in fact, we would have lost the game.

____ 4. My friend, the one with the pink hair, is coming over for dinner.

____ 5. In the end, the car wasn't a good fit for us.

____ 6. The basketball coach, Mr. Mills, cut me from the team.

TUESDAY

Match each grammar concept to its best description.

a. active voice   d. parallel structure
b. apostrophes   e. passive voice
c. colon   f. semicolon

____ 1. used when the subject receives the action

____ 2. ;

____ 3. used when a subject is completing the action

____ 4. :

____ 5. means a sentence is written to be balanced

____ 6. used to show possession and write contractions

REVIEW WEEKS 21-27

WEDNESDAY

Write your own sentence using an apostrophe correctly.

THURSDAY

Should a colon or semicolon go in the blank? Explain how you know.

The kitchen was dirty ____ however, I didn't feel like cleaning it.

FRIDAY

Correct the error(s) in the sentences. Circle your changes.

1. Rosa wore her mothers' wedding dress.

2. Jake wanted to play football, took a vacation, and buying new clothes before school started.

3. Target has several needed supplies notebooks, pens, and markers.

4. Please make sure you have your phone additionally you need your suitcase, too.

MONDAY

Circle the prepositions from the group of words below.

the   below   friends   under   in   show   at

from   to   cold   fishy   text   after   learn

beautiful   on   behind   amid   happily   by

TUESDAY

Prepositions show relationships between words in a sentence. They often show direction, time, place, location.

Ex. The cat is sleeping **on** the couch.

Finish the prepositional phrase in each sentence below.

1. Clara asked for help before _____.

2. The bell rings at _____.

3. Winter break is for _____.

4. School is from _____ to _____.

5. She lost her ring amidst _____.

6. The cat jumped into _____.

7. The family climbed aboard _____.

PREPOSITIONS and PREPOSITIONAL PHRASES

WEDNESDAY

A prepositional phrase is a phrase with a preposition, a noun or pronoun object of the preposition, and any words that modify the object. Write your own sentence including a prepositional phrase. Circle the prepositional phrase.

THURSDAY

In each sentence, the preposition is bolded. Underline the entire prepositional phrase.

1. The football team ran **across** the field.

2. She searched for the spatula **inside** the drawer.

3. The earring fell **down** the drain.

4. The puppy hid **behind** the sofa.

FRIDAY

Example: The cat is sleeping <u>**on** the couch</u>.
"On" is the preposition, and "on the couch" is the prepositional phrase that shows the location. In the sentences below, underline the prepositional phrase in each sentence and circle the preposition.

1. He sang professionally on Broadway.

2. The two dogs dug under the fence.

3. The splash pad is by the playground.

4. Jasmine loves to play at the library.

5. They unloaded the cargo near the dock.

MONDAY — What is an adjective?

A **participle** is a verbal (comes from a verb but isn't used as a verb) and usually ends in -ing, -ed, or -ed, and works as an adjective.

Circle the participle in the following sentences.

1. The crying puppy missed its mother.
2. The broken table needed to be replaced.
3. Vaughn asked his worried cousin to calm down.
4. Frowning, the teacher scolded the class.

TUESDAY

A participial phrase is a group of words that modifies a noun/pronoun. It includes a participle and any objects that go with it.

Underline the participial phrase in each sentence.

1. Leaving the mall, John drove home.
2. Julie, frowning in concentration, worked on her test.
3. Jalen noticed the dog wandering around the neighborhood.
4. Dressed in heels and a gown, Maria entered the party.
5. Chris, poking around the kitchen, looked for a snack.
6. The king angered his kingdom by taking advantage of his power.

MODIFIERS (PARTICIPLES)

WEDNESDAY

Write your own sentence with a participial phrase. Circle it.

THURSDAY

Underline the participle phrase in each sentence.

1. Being tired, Connie asks for another five minutes.

2. Collin, smiling in wonder, watched the magician.

3. Dressed in a uniform and apron, she was ready for her first shift.

FRIDAY

Dangling modifiers are participial phrases that are unclear or don't make sense in the sentence. Determine whether the following sentences have a dangling modifier. Write Y for yes and N for no.

_____ 1. Chad's brother frowned at him, looking over his sunglasses.

_____ 2. Frozen in fear, the cat meowed pitifully.

_____ 3. The doctor, sneezing loudly, woke the baby.

_____ 4. Having arrived early, waiting was required.

_____ 5. After analyzing the essay, the argument continues to be unconvincing.

MONDAY

A prefix is a word part added to the beginning of a word. A suffix is a word part added to the end of a word.

Determine what each prefix or suffix means/does to a word.

1. **un**helpful, **un**done, **un**known   **un** = _____

2. harm**less**, care**less**, worth**less**   **less** = _____

3. train**er**, teach**er**, cheat**er**   **er** = _____

4. **pre**meditate, **pre**view, **pre**heat   **pre** = _____

5. Like**able**, notice**able**, fashion**able**   **able** = _____

TUESDAY

The suffix of a word determines its part of speech. Label each suffix as a noun (**N**), verb (**V**), adjective (**ADJ**), or adverb (**ADV**).

_____ 1. temper**ate**

_____ 2. aud**ible**

_____ 3. happi**ness**

_____ 4. kin**ship**

_____ 5. happi**ly**

_____ 6. excit**ed**

_____ 7. cap**able**

_____ 8. art**ist**

_____ 9. slow**ly**

PREFIXES and SUFFIXES

WEDNESDAY

Write your own sentence using a word with a prefix/suffix and circle it.

THURSDAY

What does each prefix mean?

1. **mid**day

2. **re**do

3. **dis**agree

4. **co**exist

5. **a**typical

FRIDAY

Break each word down into its prefix, base word, and/or suffix. Some lines will be blank.

1. heaviness _____ + _____ + _____

2. nonsense _____ + _____ + _____

3. friendship _____ + _____ + _____

4. depression _____ + _____ + _____

5. misunderstanding _____ + _____ + _____

HOMOPHONES

MONDAY

Homophones are words that are spelled differently but have the same sound.

Choose the correct homophone to complete each sentence. Circle the answer.

1. (Witch/Which) one do you want?
2. It (seams/seems) like the bus isn't coming today.
3. We have a new (principal/principle) in charge this year.
4. (Whose/Who's) coming to the party?
5. The letter carrier already delivered our (male/mail).
6. Is this (your/you're) library book?

TUESDAY

Match each homophone with its best description/definition.

a. affect   d. too   g. you're
b. effect   e. two
c. to   f. your

____ 1. also, in addition

____ 2. contraction "you" + "are"

____ 3. a number

____ 4. verb (to produce an effect)

____ 5. possessive for "you"

____ 6. can be used as a preposition or added to a verb

____ 7. noun (a change that results when something happened)

WEDNESDAY

Write a sentence and include both versions of the homophone. Circle the correct one.

THURSDAY

Choose the correct homophone.

1. The (affect/effect) of your constant tardiness is a detention.

2. The (heel/heal) of her shoe broke before the dance.

3. (Their/They're/There) dog bit me.

FRIDAY

Determine whether the correct homophone is used. Write Y for yes and N for no. Fix any errors.

____ 1. The game was canceled because of the storm, to.

____ 2. You're the one she's looking for.

____ 3. I have more coffee then I can drink.

____ 4. She past the ball to her teammate.

____ 5. Give them there ball back.

____ 6. The team led in points at the half.

____ 7. She looked pail and tired, so I knew she was ill.

MONDAY

Choose which word is spelled correctly. Circle the correct answer.

1. successful vs. succesful
2. restarant vs. restaurant
3. comitted vs. committed
4. apparent vs. apparrent
5. believe vs. beleive
6. ocassion vs. occasion

TUESDAY

Choose which word is misspelled. Do your best to fix it.

1. beginning, libary, flight
   _____

2. freind, audience, principle
   _____

3. tomorow, Wednesday, compass
   _____

4. bandages, argument, branchs
   _____

5. whether, adress, disease
   _____

6. bizarre, responsability, occur
   _____

COMMONLY MISSPELLED WORDS

WEDNESDAY

Write down one thing you do to make sure you're spelling words correctly. (Don't say spell check!)

THURSDAY

What are a few words that you really struggle to spell correctly? Look them up if you need to.

FRIDAY

Choose the correct spelling of the word for the sentence. Place an X on the line for the sentence that is correct.

1. _____ The students thought the new substitute was wierd.

   _____ The students thought the new substitute was weird.

2. _____ We should feel greatful for what we have.

   _____ We should feel grateful for what we have.

3. _____ The neighborhood is growing exponentially.

   _____ The nieghborhood is growing exponentially

© Write and Read LLC 2025. All rights reserved.

MONDAY

Are the following titles capitalized and punctuated correctly? (Y or N)

____ 1. *Harry Potter And The Prisoner Of Azkaban* (book)

____ 2. As it was (song)

____ 3. "Chicago Tribune" (newspaper)

____ 4. *Stranger Things* (TV show)

____ 5. *Romeo and Juliet*

TUESDAY

Titles of long works get italicized or underlined.
Titles of short works get quotation marks.

Sort the following into being long or short works:
song · movie · magazine · poem · book/novel · short story
album · TV show · newspaper article · play · book chapter

SHORT WORKS:

LONG WORKS:

WEDNESDAY

Write a sentence using a title. Be sure to correctly capitalize and punctuate the title.

THURSDAY

What words in a title should be capitalized?

FRIDAY

Rewrite the following titles and correctly capitalize and punctuate them.

1. the most dangerous game (short story)

2. to kill a mockingbird (book)

3. chicago tribune (newspaper)

4. more people died from selfies than shark attacks (article)

5. if you were coming in the fall (poem)

MONDAY
Underline the prepositional phrase(s) in each sentence.

1. In the morning, we will go home.

2. The class filed outside during the fire drill.

3. Jayvon loves riding the horse at the grocery store.

4. Max is embarrassed by his father when leaving.

5. The three boys forgot their backpacks under the bleachers.

6. Lee found a chocolate cake inside the refrigerator.

TUESDAY
Match each grammar concept to its best description.

a. homophone   c. prefix   e. suffix
b. participle   d. preposition

____ 1. word part added to the beginning of a word

____ 2. expresses relationship to another word

____ 3. words that sound the same but are spelled differently

____ 4. word part added to the end of a word

____ 5. a word formed from a verb and used as an adjective

WEEKS 29-34 REVIEW

WEDNESDAY

Capitalize and punctuate the title of a book correctly in a sentence.

THURSDAY

What does the prefix **hyper** mean? Example: hyperactive

What does the suffix **ful** mean? Example: helpful

FRIDAY

Which sentence is written correctly? Place an X on the line to show the correct answer.

1. ____ Its almost time to celebrait your achievements.

   ____ It's almost time to celebrate your achievements.

2. ____ Crying in the bathroom, she was upset it was over.

   ____ Crying in the bathroom, upset it was over.

3. ____ They're going to see *The Bad Guys* at the movie theater.

   ____ Their going to see "The Bad Guys" at the movie theater.

MONDAY

Which sentence is written correctly? Place an X on the line.

1. ____ The coffee shop was closed so, we went to the restarant down the street.
   ____ The coffee shop was closed, so we went to the restaurant down the street.
2. ____ We saw the bus' broken wheel.
   ____ We saw the bus's broken wheel.
3. ____ The city council vote on the new bill, it doesn't pass, when they're arguing takes over.
   ____ The city council votes on the new bill; it doesn't pass when their arguing takes over.

TUESDAY

Match each word/phrase with its correct part of speech.

____ 1. beyond

____ 2. us

____ 3. soldier

____ 4. very

____ 5. distinguished

____ 6. fought

____ 7. New York City

____ 8. them

____ 9. threw

____ 10. in

a. noun

b. verb

c. adjective

d. adverb

e. preposition

f. pronoun

WHOLE YEAR REVIEW

WEDNESDAY
Write a complex sentence.

THURSDAY
Explain the difference between clauses and phrases.

FRIDAY
Rewrite each sentence to fix the errors.

1. The players goed to the new stadium and it was impressive.

2. "Whatever you want we can do" Margo promised.

3. Tommy think about what your doing, before you get in trouble.

4. Our party is on Wensday: however; we still need a lot of supplies streamers, balloons, and the cake.

5. Donald yells alot; scaredy cat; and in love with Daisy.

ANSWER KEYS

Nouns pages 6-7
Monday
The following words should be circled: horse, belief, chin, child, bones, class, grocery store, weather, hope, and textbook.
Tuesday
1. P 2. C 3. C 4. P 5. P 6. C 7. P 8. C 9. P 10. C 11. P 12. C 13. C 14. P
Wednesday
1. A 2. C 3. C 4. A 5. C 6. C 7. A 8. C 9. C 10. C 11. A 12. A
Thursday
Answers will vary.
Friday
Callie walked down to the beach, shuffling through the sand. She carried her towel and bag in her left hand. Squinting against the sun, she looked for a shady spot to sit down. Finding one, she dropped her stuff and ran to the lake.

Commas and Coordinating Conjunctions pages 8-9
Monday
1. so 2. and 3. but
Tuesday
1. no comma needed 2. packed, so 3. Cheetos, but 4. no comma needed 5. bus, yet 6. first, and
Wednesday
Answers will vary.
Thursday
F=for A=and N=nor B=but O=or Y=yet S=so
Friday
1. I, Derrick tossed the football, and Carson caught it.
2. C
3. I, Hide and Seek is Cece's favorite game but, she's not very good at it
4. C
5. C
6. I, Andrea walked home, but Steven rode his bike.

Verbs pages 10-11
Monday
The following words should be circled: hear, return, exit, accepted, remains, quieted, credit, stride, build, honor, and wash.
Tuesday
The wind howled, and rain pelted her, making her shiver. She dashed up the stairs and banged on the door. "I hope someone answers," she thought. As she shivered on the porch, she made a promise to herself. "I will find my mother someday."

ANSWER KEYS

Wednesday
1. V 2. N 3. N 4. V 5. V 6. N
Thursday
Answers will vary.
Friday

Past	Present	Future
learned	learn	will learn
pushed	push	will push
started	start	will start
cooked	cook	will cook

Capitalization pages 12-13
Monday
1. our trip to chicago was postponed after our flight from france was canceled.

2. Whenever Jaime called, officer Charles picked right up.

3. My english class was watching a movie that my ~~M~~other didn't approve of.

Tuesday
Answers will vary. Sample answers:
1. Capitalize a person's title (President Washington) but not when it's just a regular noun (the president).
2. Capitalize languages and countries. (Spain)
3. Capitalized proper nouns (Nile River) but not regular nouns (the river).
4. Capitalize the start of a sentence.

Wednesday
1. The Wind in the Willows
2. The Perks of Being a Wallflower
3. The Catcher in the Rye

Thursday
Answers will vary.

Friday
1. ____ Where is the President?
   _X_ Where is the president?
2. _X_ We'll go visit Lake Michigan this summer.
   ____ We'll go visit lake Michigan this summer.
3. ____ Maddie's taking english and french this year.
   _X_ Maddie's taking English and French this year.

ANSWER KEYS

Pronouns pages 14-15
Monday
1. its 2. his 3. I 4. We 5. their
Tuesday
The following should be underlined in each sentence.
1. My mother and I
2. Nathan
3. The team
4. Arnold
5. The members of Congress
6. Andre
7. Mia and Emma
Wednesday
Sample answers:
Subject: I, he, she, you, we, they, it
Object: me, him, her, you, us, them, it
Thursday
Answers will vary.
Friday
1. their 2. her 3. its 4. my 5. their 6. his

Subject and Predicate pages 16-17
Monday
The following words should be circled.
1. The big black dog
2. Sam
3. Jadan, my best friend
Tuesday
1. The novel ended with a twist.
2. Polly the parakeet flew through the enclosure, looking for a place to land.
3. Eventually, our class will finish the final project.
4. The earthquake rattled the windows.
Wednesday
Answers will vary.
Thursday
Answers will vary.
Friday
Answers will vary, but they need to follow this guide.
1. The answer needs to be a noun or pronoun.
2. The answer needs to be a noun or pronoun.
3. The answer needs to include a verb and what's happening to it.
4. The answer needs to include a verb and what's happening to it.

Independent Clauses pages 18-19
Monday
An independent clause has a subject and predicate and is a complete thought.
Tuesday
1. N 2. I 3. I 4. N 5. I 6. N 7. I 8. I 9. N 10. I

ANSWER KEYS

Wednesday
While it has a subject and a predicate, it cannot stand alone as a sentence due to the word "if."
Thursday
Answers will vary.
Friday
Answers will vary. Sample answers:
1. The great debate was held in the auditorium.
2. After her tantrum, she was tired and took a nap.
3. Breaking down the boxes took us two hours.
4. She's had nightmares since she read the book.

Simple and Compound Sentences pages 20-21
Monday
Simple Sentence: It has one independent clause.
Compound Sentence: It has two or more independent clauses.
Tuesday
1. C 2. S 3. S 4. C 5. C 6. C 7. C 8. S 9. S
Wednesday
Answers will vary.
Thursday
You can use a comma and coordinating conjunction. You could also use a semicolon.
Friday
1. N, Cal asked Patrice out, but she said no.
2. Y
3. N, The restaurant was closed, so we went somewhere else.
4. N, Jesus made the baseball team his freshman year; his family was very proud. *or* Jesus made the baseball team his freshman year, and his family was very proud.
5. Y

Sentence Fragments and Run-On Sentences pages 22-23
Monday
Sentence Fragment: It is an incomplete sentence missing either its subject or a complete predicate.
Run-On Sentence: It is multiple independent clauses put together without proper punctuation.
Tuesday
1. SF 2. SF 3. RO 4. RO 5. SF 6. RO 7. RO 8. SF
Wednesday
Zane slid to home plate, but the catcher got him out. It was a run-on sentence because it was missing the comma and coordinating conjunction.
Thursday
Answers will vary, but it needs a subject and verb added.
Friday
1. C 2. RO 3. SF 4. SF 5. C 6. RO

Weeks 1-9 Review pages 24-25
Monday
Answers will vary.

ANSWER KEYS

Tuesday
1. D 2. F 3. A 4. B 5. C 6. E
Wednesday
Answers will vary.
Thursday

(Gary) handed (Susan) the (umbrella) when it started to rain. (Susan) smiled and thanked him. (Gary) smiled back.

Friday
1. C 2. F 3. S 4. C 5. S 6. S

Dependent Clauses pages 26-27
Monday
Independent Clause: It has a subject and predicate and can stand alone as a sentence.
Dependent Clause: It has a subject and predicate, but it can't stand alone as a sentence. It's dependent on more information.
1. Y 2. N 3. Y
Tuesday
1. After Carla failed her test, she asked if she could retake it.
2. The football game was canceled since a thunderstorm rolled in.
3. The students voted to read outside because the weather was finally nice.
4. Even though the team lost, everyone was proud of the players' progress.
5. The receptionist will keep your ID until you return.
Wednesday
Answers will vary
Thursday
"Whenever" keeps it from being a complete thought, but there is a subject (she) and predicate (calls).
Friday
1. D 2. I 3. I 4. D 5. D 6. D

Clauses and Phrases
Monday
They both have a subject and predicate.
1. Y (It's missing the subject and linking verb.)
2. N (subject: I, predicate: called yesterday)
Tuesday
1. P 2. C 3. C 4. P 5. P 6. P 7. C 8. C 9. C
Wednesday
Answers will vary. Ensure there isn't a subject and predicate, and the explanation should include that.
Thursday
Circle: In the beginning
Underline: Carla didn't need help

ANSWER KEYS

Friday
1. P 2. D 3. D 4. I 5. P 6. I

Complex Sentences pages 30-31
Monday
Simple Sentence: It has one independent clause.
Compound Sentence: It has two independent clauses.
Complex Sentence: It has an independent clause and a dependent clause.
Tuesday
1. Y 2. Y 3. N 4. N 5. N 6. Y 7. Y
Wednesday
Answers will vary.
Thursday
Underline: Betty's mother forced her to go
Circle: though she didn't want to
Friday
1. Y 2. Y 3. N 4. Y 5. N

Compound-Complex Sentences pages 32-33
Monday
A compound-complex sentence has at least two independent clauses and at least one dependent clause.
Tuesday
1. N 2. Y 3. N 4. Y 5. Y 6. N
Wednesday
Answers will vary.
Thursday
No, there needs to be a comma after "cold" between the first independent clause (with dependent) and the second independent clause.
Friday
1. CC 2. S 3. C 4. CX 5. CX 6. CC

Subject/Verb Agreement pages 34-35
Monday
1. speaks 2. think 3. believe 4. prefers 5. smell
Tuesday
1. Y 2. N 3. Y 4. N 5. N 6. Y
Wednesday
Answers will vary.
Thursday
No, Sarah is singular, so the verb needs an "s" at the end.
Friday
1. looks 2. need 3. exits 4. requires 5. dies 6. want

Types of Verbs pages 36-37
Monday
1. appeared 2. smells 3. is

ANSWER KEYS

Tuesday
1. The track team (ran) at practice.

2. The postman (delivered) the mail.

3. The birds (might build) a nest here again.

4. Olive (is obsessed) with her stuffed dog.

Wednesday
Answers will vary.
Thursday
"Is" is a linking verb connecting Bobby to fan.
Friday
1. H 2. L 3. A 4. L 5. H 6. A

Irregular Verbs pages 38-39
Monday
The following words should be circled: begin, is, know, run, steal, and swim.
Tuesday
1. broke 2. read 3. woke 4. led 5. blew, left 6. felt, made 7. see, has, fallen 8. was, sing
Wednesday
Answers will vary.
Thursday
1. possible answers: built, had, chose, found, kept
2. possible answers: slept, ate, fell
Friday
1. was 2. cut 3. sold 4. slept 5. took 6. won 7. bought 8. caught 9. drank 10. found 11. paid 12. stole

Commas 1 pages 40-41
Monday
Answers will vary. Sample answers:
1. Use a comma between the day and year and after the full date to set it off from the rest of the sentence. (Ex. May 15, 1982, is my parents' anniversary.)
2. Use a comma between the city and state and after the state to set it off from the rest of the sentence. (Ex. The Post Office is located at 125 Main Street, Lincoln, Kansas.)
3. If two adjectives next to each other are of equal importance, use a comma between them. (Ex. The grouchy, tired man lost his temper.)
Tuesday
1. The Declaration of Independence was adopted on July 4, 1776, which makes it an important day in US history.
2. I want to go to Los Angeles, California one day.
3. The black, fluffy dog was very friendly.
4. As I read the sign, I realized we need to stop for gas before we cross the long bridge.
5. Natalie was really excited about the party, so she invited extra people.
6. Although I understood the directions, I did not follow them.

ANSWER KEYS

Wednesday
Answers will vary.
Thursday
If two adjectives next to each other are of equal importance, use a comma between them.
Friday
1. _____ Bobby's license says his birthdate is September 15, 2002 but he's always told me his birthday is the 16th.
   __X__ Bobby's license says his birthdate is September 15, 2002, but he's always told me his birthday is the 16th.
2. __X__ Though Charlotte is from Baton Rouge, Louisiana, you'd never know it from the way she talks.
   _____ Though Charlotte is from Baton Rouge, Louisiana you'd never know it from the way she talks.
3. __X__ Violet wants an updated cell phone.
   _____ Violet wants an updated, cell phone.

Adjectives and Adverbs pages 42-43
Monday
1. The (old) man walked (tiredly) down the stairs.

2. (Tomorrow), Ronnie will pick up the puppy.

3. Alejandro ran (quickly) around the track.

4. The (blue) sky was (clear).

5. Wren sang (beautifully).

Tuesday
1. adj 2. adv 3. adv 4. adj 5. adj 6. adv 7. adv 8. adj
Wednesday
Answers will vary.
Thursday
It is an adverb, and it is modifying bright.
Friday
1. well 2. bad 3. really 4. good 5. badly
Good and bad are adjectives. Well and badly are adverbs.

Weeks 11-19 Review pages 44 and 45
Monday
1. H 2. A 3. L 4. A 5. H 6. L
Tuesday
1. E 2. D 3. F 4. B 5. C 6. A
Wednesday
Answers will vary.
Thursday
1. The dog or the cat needs to ride in the backseat.

ANSWER KEYS

2. The dogs bark loudly.
3. The cat cries when it is cold.
Friday
1. _____ The table breaked after the heavy wooden fan fell on it.
   __X__ The table broke after the heavy, wooden fan fell on it.
2. _____ April 15, is Tax Day in the US, but my mother and father forgets every year.
   __X__ April 15 is Tax Day in the US, but my mother and father forget every year.
3. _____ His uncle asked for his help after school, though he had other plans, he said okay.
   __X__ His uncle asked for his help after school; though he had other plans, he said okay.

Semicolons pages 46-47
Monday
1. ; It looks like a comma with a period over it.
2. It's connecting two independent clauses with a conjunctive adverb (however).
Tuesday
1. I'd like to visit Los Angeles, California; Seattle, Washington; and Phoenix, Arizona next summer.
2. When we finally leave, please call your uncle; he's going to be worried.
3. Josh is getting his first dog; therefore, he needs a lot of new supplies.
4. Chris came home early; his car got a flat tire.
5. I need eggs, for your breakfast tomorrow; fish; and butter, in case ours is melted.
Wednesday
Answers will vary.
Thursday
One of the items in the list (new, green coat) contains a comma.
Friday
1. No: I'm going to order coffee, orange juice, and french toast for breakfast.
2. No: The photographer ruined the pictures; as a result, the client refused to pay.
3. Yes
4. No: Bianca asked her parents for an advance on her allowance, but they refused.
5. Yes
6. No: Xavier wanted to join the team, but he couldn't practice on Tuesdays.

Colons pages 48-49
Monday
A colon looks like a period on top of a period. :
1. My grandfather gave the best advice: "Be ambitious, be flexible, and be happy."
2. You need the following things for practice: cleats, jersey, and water bottle.
3. The recipe calls for a 2:1 ratio of water to rice.
Tuesday
1. Use a colon to express a ratio.
2. Use a colon to set off a quote if what comes before the quote is an independent clause.
3. Use a colon to set off a list if what comes before the list is an independent clause.
Wednesday
Answers will vary.
Thursday
Use a colon to set off a list if what comes before the list is an independent clause.

ANSWER KEYS

Friday
1. _____ You need: notebooks, pencils, and folders.
   __X__ You need to take the following things: notebooks, pencils, and folders.
2. __X__ He yelled, "I love you!"
   _____ He yelled; "I love you!"
3. _____ I tell my students this all the time; "Following directions is a life skill."
   __X__ I tell my students this all the time: "Following directions is a life skill."

Quotation Marks pages 50-51
Monday
Quotation marks are used to show that someone is talking or that the material comes from someone else.
1. Mr. Barkley yelled, "Get out of my garden!"
2. "I'm afraid the kitchen is closed," the waiter told us.
3.1.Destiny explained, "A mouse chewed through the wires."
Tuesday
1. The director barked, "Get out here this instant!"
2. "The show must go on," he declared.
3. "Please," Wanda pleaded, "don't leave me here."
4. Chester called, "Come here, kitty."
Wednesday
Answers will vary.
Thursday
The punctuation goes inside the quotation marks to show that it's connected to that text, not necessarily what comes after it.
Friday
1. N 2. Y 3. Y 4. N 5. Y

Apostrophes pages 52-53
Monday
1. the choir's
2. princess's
3. classes'
4. Anna's
5. parents'
6. horse's
7. team's
8. boss's
9. Mr. Wells's
10. men's
11. princesses'
12. Mrs. Reynolds'

Tuesday
1. it is 2. could not 3. will not *or* would not 4. I am 5. they have 6. you all 7. she would *or* she had 8. you have 9. we had 10. have not
Wednesday
Answers will vary.
Thursday
1. aren't 2. he's 3. won't 4. I'll 5. wouldn't 6. we'll
Friday
1. N 2. N 3. Y 4. Y 5. Y 6. N

ANSWER KEYS

Commas 2 pages 54-55

Monday
1. Appositive phrases rename a noun/pronoun and need to be set off with commas.
2. Set off introductory and transition words or phrases with a comma.
3. Interrupting words or phrases interrupt the general flow of the sentence. These words or phrases can be removed without affecting the overall structure of the sentence and must be set off with commas as a result.

Tuesday
1. No: Consequently, you didn't get the job.
2. Yes
3. Yes
4. No: She wondered, however, if anyone else knew.
5. No: Patty, the one with the new car, wants to hire a new maid.
6. No: Like I said, no, you didn't get the job.
7. No: Leah, the girl with the ponytail, is a great diver.

Wednesday
Answers will vary

Thursday
It's an appositive phrase. "The new student" is renamed as "Taylor" and needs to be set off by commas.

Friday
1. In addition, make sure you correct the following issues.
2. Our waiter, the one with the long hair, is over by the kitchen.
3. Plenty of people, in fact, don't believe it.
4. You and I, therefore, are no longer friends.
5. Yesterday, the cat ran away.
6. Chris Evans, who played Captain America in the Marvel movies, is his favorite actor.

Parallel Structure pages 56-57

Monday
1. _____ I need to buy groceries, stopping by the post office, and returned library books.
   __X__ I need to buy groceries, stop by the post office, and return library books.
2. __X__ The girl sang beautifully and clearly.
   _____ The girl sang beautifully and also clearly.
3. _____ When she called, he will let me know.
   __X__ When she called, he let me know.

Tuesday
1. Carlos would like a new phone and a new tablet.
2. Vanessa hates to run and to swim. *or* Vanessa hates running and swimming.
3. Carrot is an older, orange cat.
4. Abby likes reading books, building with blocks, and singing the ABC's.

Wednesday
Answers will vary.

Thursday
Answers may vary. Sample answer: Parallel structure makes sure all parts of the sentence match.

ANSWER KEYS

Friday
1. No: Her cousin enjoys hiking at the Dunes and swimming in Lake Michigan.
2. Yes
3. Yes
4. No: Bob practices on Tuesdays, Thursdays, and Saturdays.
5. Yes
6. No: Ollie loves cupcakes, cookies, and pies.

Active vs. Passive Voice pages 58-59
Monday
1. A 2. P 3.P 4.A 5. A
Tuesday
1. They cleaned the house before it sold.
2. We lost the puzzle pieces while putting it away.
3. Our dinner was delivered by UberEats.
4. The plane's takeoff was almost an hour late.
Wednesday
Answers will vary.
Thursday
The sentence is active. The subject of the sentence (Barbara) does the action.
Friday
1. __X__ My brother invited me to his wedding.
   _____ I was invited by my brother to his wedding.
2. _____ Someone robbed our house last night.
   __X__ Our house was robbed last night.
3. __X__ Walter needs to buy new school supplies.
   _____ New school supplies are needed by Walter.

Review Weeks 21-27 pages 60-61
Monday
1. C 2. B 3. C 4. A 5. B 6. A
Tuesday
1. E 2. F 3. A 4. C 5. D 6. B
Wednesday
Answers will vary.
Thursday
The sentence should use a semicolon because it joins two independent clauses.
Friday
1. Rosa wore her mother's wedding dress.

2. Jake wanted to play football, take a vacation, and buy new clothes before school started.

3. Target has several needed supplies: notebooks, pens, and markers.

4. Please make sure you have your phone; additionally, you need your suitcase, too.

ANSWER KEYS

Prepositions and Prepositional Phrases pages 62-63
Monday
The following words should be circled: below, under, in, at, from, to, after, on, behind, amid, by
Tuesday
Answers will vary. Sample answers:
1. Clara asked for help before the bell rang.
2. The bell rings at 2:35 p.m.
3. Winter break is for rest and relaxation.
4. School is from 7:30 to 2:30.
5. She lost her ring amidst the weeds.
6. The cat jumped into the shoe box.
7. The family climbed aboard the cruise ship.
Wednesday
Answers will vary.
Thursday
1. The football team ran **across** the field.
2. She searched for the spatula **inside** the drawer.
3. The earring fell **down** the drain.
4. The puppy hid **behind** the sofa.
Friday
1. He sang professionally on Broadway.

2. The two dogs dug under the fence.

3. The splash pad is by the playground.

4. Jasmine loves to play at the library.

5. They unloaded the cargo near the dock.

Modifiers (Participles) pages 64-65
Monday
An adjective is a word that describes/modifies a noun or pronoun.
1. crying 2. broken 3. worried 4. frowning
Tuesday
1. Leaving the mall, John drove home.
2. Julie, frowning in concentration, worked on her test.
3. Jalen noticed the dog wandering around the neighborhood.
4. Dressed in heels and a gown, Maria entered the party.
5. Chris, poking around the kitchen, looked for a snack.
6. The king angered his kingdom by taking advantage of his power.
Wednesday
Answers will vary.
Thursday
1. Being tired, Connie asks for another five minutes.
2. Collin, smiling in wonder, watched the magician.
3. Dressed in a uniform and apron, she was ready for her first shift.

ANSWER KEYS

Friday
1. Yes: We don't know who is looking.
2. N
3. N
4. Yes: We don't know who or what is waiting.
5. Yes: We don't know who analyzed the essay.

Prefixes and Suffixes pages 66-67
Monday
1. not 2. without 3. a person who does something 4. before 5. has that trait
Tuesday
1. ADJ 2. ADJ 3. N 4. N 5. ADV 6. V 7. ADJ 8. N 9. ADV
Wednesday
Answers will vary.
Thursday
1. middle 2. again 3. not 4. with or together 5. not or without
Friday
1. heaviness= _____ + heavy + ness
2. nonsense= non + sense + _____
3. friendship= _____ + friend + ship
4. depression= de + press + ion
5. misunderstanding= mis + understand + ing

Homophones pages 68-69
Monday
1. Which 2. seems 3. principal 4. Who's 5. mail 6. your
Tuesday
1. D 2. G 3. E 4. A 5. F 6. C 7. B
Wednesday
Answers will vary.
Thursday
1. effect 2. heel 3. Their
Friday
1. No: The game was canceled because of the storm, **too**.
2. Yes
3. No: I have more coffee **than** I can drink.
4. No: She **passed** the ball to her teammate.
5. No: Give them **their** ball back.
6. Yes
7. No: She looked **pale** and tired, so I knew she was ill.

Commonly Misspelled Words pages 70-71
Monday
1. successful vs. succesful
2. restarant vs. restaurant
3. comitted vs. committed

ANSWER KEYS

4. (apparent) vs. apparrent
5. (believe) vs. beleive
6. ocassion vs. (occasion)

Tuesday
1. library 2. friend 3. tomorrow 4. branches 5. address 6. responsibility

Wednesday
Answers will vary.

Thursday
Answers will vary.

Friday
1. _____ The students thought the new substitute was wierd.
   __X__ The students thought the new substitute was weird.
2. _____ We should feel greatful for what we have.
   __X__ We should feel grateful for what we have.
3. __X__ The neighborhood is growing exponentially.
   _____ The nieghborhood is growing exponentially

Titles pages 72-73

Monday
1. No 2. No 3. No 4. Yes 5. Yes

Tuesday
Short Works: song, poem, short story, newspaper article, book chapter
Long Works: movie, magazine, book/novel, album, TV show, play

Wednesday
Answers will vary.

Thursday
The first, last, and all important words.

Friday
1. "The Most Dangerous Game"
2. If handwritten: To Kill a Mockingbird If typed: *To Kill a Mockingbird*
3. If handwritten: Chicago Tribune If typed: *Chicago Tribune*
4. "More People Died from Selfies than Shark Attacks"
5. "If You Were Coming in the Fall"

Weeks 29-34 Review pages 74-75

Monday
1. In the morning, we will go home.
2. The class filed outside during the fire drill.
3. Jayvon loves riding the horse at the grocery store.
4. Max is embarrassed by his father when leaving.
5. The three boys forgot their backpacks under the bleachers.
6. Lee found a chocolate cake inside the refrigerator.

Tuesday
1. C 2. D 3. A 4. E 5. B

Wednesday
Answers will vary.

ANSWER KEYS

Thursday

Hyper means extreme. Ful shows possession of a quality.

Friday

1. ___ Its almost time to celebrait your achievements.
   _X_ It's almost time to celebrate your achievements.
2. _X_ Crying in the bathroom, she was upset it was over.
   ___ Crying in the bathroom, upset it was over.
3. _X_ They're going to see *The Bad Guys* at the movie theater.
   ___ Their going to see "The Bad Guys" at the movie theater.

Whole Year Review pages 76-77

Monday

1. ___ The coffee shop was closed so, we went to the restarant down the street.
   _X_ The coffee shop was closed, so we went to the restaurant down the street.
2. ___ We saw the bus' broken wheel.
   _X_ We saw the bus's broken wheel.
3. ___ The city council vote on the new bill, it doesn't pass, when they're arguing takes over.
   _X_ The city council votes on the new bill; it doesn't pass when their arguing takes over.

Tuesday

1. E 2. F 3. A 4. D 5. C 6. B 7. A 8. F 9. B 10. E

Wednesday

Answers will vary.

Thursday

Clauses and phrases have a subject and predicate. Phrases do not.

Friday

1. The players went to the new stadium, and it was impressive.
2. "Whatever you want, we can do," Margo promised.
3. Tommy, think about what you're doing before you get in trouble.
4. Our party is on Wednesday, however, we still need a lot of supplies: streamers, balloons, and the cake.
5. Answers will vary. Sample: Donald yells a lot, is a scaredy cat, and loves Daisy.

Copyrighted Materials: All Rights Reserved
© Write and Read LLC 2024

Connect with the author:
writeandreadteacher.com
@writeandreadteacher

Made in the USA
Las Vegas, NV
10 August 2025